T0195821

Eagle
A New symbol of African American Rebirth

THE PILGRIMAGE

African American's Rebirth

OKSEN BABAKHANIAN

authorHOUSE®

AuthorHouse™
1663 Liberty Drive
Bloomington, IN 47403
www.authorhouse.com
Phone: 833-262-8899

Published by AuthorHouse 04/16/2021

ISBN: 978-1-6655-2227-4 (sc)
ISBN: 978-1-6655-2225-0 (hc)
ISBN: 978-1-6655-2226-7 (e)

Library of Congress Control Number: 2021907252

Print information available on the last page.

Oksen Babakhanian

In collaboration with Ailin Babakhanian

This Manifesto is to revolutionize African Americans culture and mindset of slavery and bondage to a freedom that comes from the heart and mind and flow to reality of life, a life of freedom and respect for the soul of the African Americans.

Oksen Babakhanian

In collaboration with **Ailin Babakhanian**

The Pilgrimage

African Americans' *Rebirth*

This book is about my love and passion for African Americans who as slaves, came to the shores of America in 1619 and although they are free citizens today, but their color has been associated with their slave mentality and it is with us and ongoing. We need to do something to bring equality of blacks and whites in our country so we can see everybody in the light of who they are, not what the color of their skins are.

CONTENTS

PREFACE

I have immigrated to The United States of America in mid 1970s, to Oklahoma City, Oklahoma, as a student in Oklahoma University. I was so proud to be in America and be part of the American dream. I enjoyed my moments with my fellow American students and the people in the small city of Norman, Oklahoma. But the view was changed after a few years, when I was working in Oklahoma City and got to know the city itself. The northeast was all blacks, northwest was where rich people lived, southwest and southeast the regular white people lived, which sometimes were called "Rednecks." This division of the city really bothered me a lot. And I heard from my coworkers that I should not travel to the black areas because it was dangerous. Having the dream that America was a land of opportunities, and a beacon of progress, democratic values, and appreciation of the rights of every human being, but the notion of the segregation between blacks and whites was bothersome. After learning history of America, and the period of slavery and after the emancipation of freedom for blacks but still I could see the segregation even up to today. After finishing my bachelor's degree in engineering from the university of Oklahoma, I moved to Los Angeles, California, and I have been living with my family up to now. During my working years, I have learned more about the culture of black people, their life styles and sadly all the discriminations that they are still going through, and most of the jails are filled with black prisoners with a huge percentages compared to other races. Recently, I had a chance to read a book named "Beloved", by Toni Morrison, which had a tremendous effect on me. After that, being a retired engineer, I started to think and study more about slavery and the situations and the culture of the black people. I had lots of questions in my mind about behavior and culture of black people and tremendous discrimination they received from their white fellow citizens.

FREEDOM

Freedom is the word that is mentioned, talked about, dreamed about and fight for it, countries have gone to war for it and millions of people have died yearning for freedom. Freedom is the innermost feeling that human beings must be fulfilled and dreamed during ages, to be free of personal and environmental restrictions. It looks like when God created human being, he installed this yearning into the man so he can always dream higher, work harder to reach that plateau of freedom where he can breathe fresh air and think himself of the master of the world of his surrounding and nobody can restrict him of movement. Even animals and other specious have this urge to be free to fly or to swim or run any directions they want without any restrictions or blockage. Freedom is a feeling and the space that people feel in control of themselves and their destiny. Freedom could be as individual for a single human being or for the group of people, nations, nationalities, and countries themselves. Therefore, it is for this purpose; meaning attaining our freedom, that makes us work hard, excel, and try anything in our power to reach that plateau. We use our intelligence or strength or weaponry and most of all God to help us in this journey. The call for freedom is a universal one and all mankind from all corners of the world have been yearning for it for centuries. Countries have gone for wars to get their freedoms. Slaves have fought, cheated and run away; they have killed the slave holders so they can be free. Freedom is that fresh air and highest of the feeling one gets when he is free to do whatever he wants to. That moment of freedom is so precious that when you get it at first you are over whelmed and it takes time to sink in the feeling, like the eagle who is trapped and kept in a cage for years, one day you open the cage door and you let her out and you wait for her to fly... at first for few moments... it seems years she stays put. Just moves her wings but not flying, it seems she is dumb funded or she cannot believe her eyes the open air... the blue sky... the shining sun, the mountains, the trees... so many places, such a vastness, big world... Freedom...Freedom at last... free to fly, to go, to do whatever she wants...the appealing surge, the crisp air under the belly, moving the wings free... the cage is open, nobody is staring at you, nobody says a word, nobody to call your name black... Niger... beautiful or ugly... nobody tries to make you laugh or sing when you want to cry...nobody to admire your petty life in the cage... oh what a pity... nobody to teach you strange songs with the crappie voices, young and old trying to teach you something... things you do not know or want to know, because it is not in your nature, it is not you... why they put you in cage...why they try to make a mockery of all who you are in your world... why they slave you for their entertainment or abuse... Why... Why... Why... mom! Mom I cannot breathe... you are killing me...let me loose... let me go... let me fly from this cage... what did I do to you to deserve this...why... why...why I am enslaved... When I did not do any harm to you and your family...why...why keeping me in this damn cage...your pity look...your ugly dirty hands feeding me... I cannot breathe... mom...mom... oh when you touch me with your filthy hands full of microbes and dirt, try to suit me, smooth my wings, oh I cannot breath... the dirty hands feeding me and your children playing with me, squeeze the life out of me, why... they laugh when I cry from my pain, why... freedom...fresh air... nobody to stare or squeeze my body, nobody to force me to sing while I am crying inside.... Freedom... blue sky...the world is mine and I am the king...I can fly...thank you God. Thank you for letting me be free from my cage... from my slavery, I can fly now, I can laugh and cry when I want to. I will be hungry but heck no problem… nobody squeezes the life out of me. I will try with my own will. I will find food and be happy with little food in freedom.

PILGRIMING TO MECCA

Why Muslims go to Mecca every year? Because to get strength and energized by Muslim religious faith and activity. That is why millions of Muslims go to Haj and Mecca every year.

People dream about the pilgrimage; they work hard for few years to save money for the trip. This trip and pilgrimage is so uplifting and has such a great effect on those people that they carry this memory for their lifetime and they add a prefix to their name, such as "Haji" which means, they have gone to the Haj for the pilgrimage to show their faith and belief in the Muslim religion. This act of going to Hajj makes those people much more religious, hardworking, faithful citizens who are enormously proud of their accomplishments and saver their name tag "Haji." These people change their attitude toward the fellow citizens and have more respect and care for them. Likewise, the citizens themselves who have not gone to the pilgrimage, will show immense respect and honor to those who have gone the pilgrimage and they always wish they can do this trip hopefully next year. They try harder to save money for pilgrimage budget and they are more eager to go thru many sacrifices in order to accomplish their lifelong wish. With this example, it is obvious that if African Americans (black American?) are taught to work hard and prepare to travel to Africa to the lands of forefathers would be an immense revelation and enlightening for them to see black African like them which never been slaved and are free and proud citizens of their country. This revelation will change the attitude and the culture of African Americans to be positive, proud, and never go back to the culture of slavery, homelessness and lack of responsibility for their families.

Those who come back from pilgrimage become more religious, more caring toward their fellow citizens no matter what their skin color is. They try to act more like the free and strong fellow Africans with proud and an immense feeling of love and care toward their families and the society. They will try to not submit to old way of life of destitute and shamelessness. They will not have the heavy burden of slave mentality or carrier of feelings of injustice, which they were overburdened before.

PILGRIMING
TO ARMENIA
(A PERSONAL STORY)

When I go to Armenia, which is every summer, I get rejuvenated, get more energy and sense of belonging and proud to be part of Armenian culture, and feel complete and ready to be a productive citizen even though living in America. I have been born in Iran, in an Armenian family. My ancestors are Armenians who were brought to Iran in the 1600s by Shah Abbas, the Iranian king. He uprooted thousands of Armenians from Armenia, brought to Isfahan the capital of Persia, during the war with Turkey. The Shah had in mind that since Armenians are well cultured and industrialized nation, they could revitalize the industry and trade in Iran.

In 1973, I traveled to USA for my university education. After the graduation I stayed, worked and became a US citizen. I established my own Structural Engineering and Design office for more than a quarter century.

When I go to Armenia, I feel great, and twice as strong with the power to do everything. In Armenia, wherever you look you see Armenians just like yourself, you feel you are among your brothers and sisters, with warmth closeness and appreciating being an Armenian. When I visited the tomb of one of our old kings, "King Ashot Yerkat" The Iron Feast Ashot, I had goosebumps all over seeing the majestic site of our beloved king's tomb laying in front of me. The feeling was so great and satisfying and I was so proud to have a king like him in our history and I was twice as much amazed that I could feel his presence and imagining I was living in Armenia in his time, a proud Armenian with a strong king.

When I Returned back to the States, I was more proud to be Armenian in USA and tried to do my job the best I could, to honor my ancestors and, also I was more polite and humble toward my fellow American citizens. I respected them more, so they would reciprocate the same toward me and we would have a very cordial relationship.

PILGRIMING TO AFRICA

Imagine the joy and the wonder that a black family puts steps on the African soil. They see black people all around them with these beautiful colorful dresses, with big smiles and laughter which pronounce the freedom, strength and happiness that a free person can feel. The families are in shock... It is amazing to see so many black people just like yourself and you as a part of them, you feel great, you feel warm, you feel like you are walking in the sky... you feel the strength and happiness of your surroundings, you're not alone anymore. You have people like you all around whispering, talking, laughing as if nothing else is important...no bills... no cups around...no drug dealing...no fights between family members for nothing special, just calling each other bitch. No respect, no shame and reverence for people around just using the cussing words as loud as they can without regard to neighbors or their own family. Here in Africa, people are quiet, they are not fighting for nothing, they are not cussing each other loudly, they are just ordinary people walking proudly with joy doing their daily chores. you feel like it is another planet it has nothing to do where you came from… the houses is different… the cars is different, very old… the clothes they wear… their shoes everything are different but their black faces…you see even the blackness on their face is not intimidating anymore it is warm, it is human, it's like you inside when you are alone… when there is no body specially no white people around… you feel calm, you feel great inside, you want to cry loud that everybody can see and hear, it the cry of happiness and joy it's cry of freedom… it's a cry of being among yourself, then you want to laugh, you want to laugh so loud that the whole city can hear you! They can feel your joy inside and out, they can feel your call of freedom, a free man at last with no regrets, with no shame on his face, a face which has been different and shameful and heartbreaks all over where he came from. Now he is a man with full of warmth, full of love, and empathy for fellow citizens, he cares about all and everything is good… everything is palpable and he is content… he's not the black in the white surrounding. He is not the object of shame anymore; he is not walking down or slow or scared of the cups and others and he is proud now to be who he is without color. In Africa, you feel like an ordinary person with an ordinary family, working hard and make your life the best you can with a job that you have and be a respectful citizen of the country like anywhere else in any other country. You have your ups and downs but at the end of the day you have your family and your neighbors to appreciate and be thankful for the things God has provided for you. You are free person like anybody else to go through the life with all it is miseries and happiness but with no shames and nobody to frown on you just because of your skin color. In Africa, you do not feel or see the blackness on people's face of hands or feet... all you see is another human beings just like you who wants to live and enjoy the life, work hard and be proud of what he has accomplished. He goes to church not as a wounded person but as a proud member of the society who goes to church to pray and thank God for all he has given him. He is not bitter because of his skin color. He is just thankful for his family's health and asks God to forgive his misgivings and more strength to do his daily chores.

BAD NEWS
(ANOTHER SHOOTING)

In the United States of America, there is not a day that goes by that we do not hear another police shooting of a black person. It is heart reaching to hear all those shootings of black people by mostly white police officers. The minute a white police man sees a black man doing something wrong, it's either drug dealing or domestic disturbances right then in his mind already judges that the black man is guilty and he has to stop him in any possible way and especially shooting to death because he does not want him to be alive and sue him for wrongdoing. This phenomenon in police stations through out the country is the norm and it is the environment in those white policemen are trained to be tough and not forgiving when it comes to black criminals and felons. Historically there is always been a bias toward the black people, since the day the slave ships brought those black Africans to American shores, white people has always been afraid of black slaves as it is we have the fear of the night darkness. Therefore, the white people have always looked at blacks with suspicion and fear even though the poor black man did not do anything wrong, his color has a guilty sign on it that when a white person looks at it, has already determined the guilt and judged accordingly. Imagine the anguish and heartbreaks and trauma that a black family feels when there is another shooting in magazines or media because they all know well that one of them got shot again, it might be their husband, son, father, friend or town's people. Can you imagine a black child who is growing up in an environment of fear, hate, fatherlessness, and humiliation that he feels in class, in shopping centers, while driving or sitting in a restaurant when others look at you with a look of misery, suspicion, and fear in their eyes. In such an environment how can we expect to see this young black acting perfectly as if nothing has happened, he has brought up in a warm family in the suburbs or in the city without knowing the pain and humiliations that he has gone through and he still going to the same ordeals even today. It is the time and passed the time that we as Americans study, do the research and once for all, the people and government together change the way we treat our black citizens and teach our police officers to not look at the color of the person as the felon but to look all citizens equally, without the color to judge the person or his guilt till proven guilty in the court. We need to associate with our black neighbors as equals and not look at their color for determining their sincerity, or guilt.

RIOTS

And there are those Riots every few years in different states, cities of our country! And usually it starts with the shooting of a black person by a white police officer. The Riots starts because of black citizens of that city by knowing the nature of killing and most of the time the way the person is gone down by police make those black communities to uprise and get mad because of all the injustices that they have themselves have gone through and they feel empathy and outrage by hearing another shooting, another black person dead on the floor. Those black people to try to get their voice heard, so they do the riots. They come out in groups, they shout, and they call and cuss the cups and they break store doors and windows, smash cars, and anything they can get their hands on to express their anger and frustration. Sometimes they start shooting and some bystanders are getting hurt by those rioters. The media and lots of law enforcement right of the batt, they call those rioters, hooligans, and criminals because they are disturbing the peace and damaging shops and stealing goods from them. Most people look at those riots with hate towards the blacks and they call them thieves and criminals without really analyzing the situation and having compassion for those rioters who come out of desperation and injustices that they feel all their life. This is the way they show their utmost pain and suffering that they have gone through their whole life because they were born black and they are sons and daughters of those slaves who were brought to the shore of America in 1619. To eliminate these riots, the government and media should start talking about those issues and not blaming that. They should think and come up with legislation and do a thorough study of the black issues and try to solve once for all this condition so there would not be riots anymore. The police need to be trained to do their jobs better, and not be intimidated by black citizens or felons. They should study the situation, make it calm and decide accordingly not in a haste. People should understand that there is a hidden and a history behind those riots therefore it needs careful study and change in the thinking and attitude of people of the black race.

HOMELESSNESS

It is sad and shameful that in the twenty-first century in America, this great land of freedom and abundance we see homeless people all over in our neighborhoods. It is a tragedy that we as a civilized nation with money and wealth and knowhow and the technical progress in every aspect of society with doctors and sociologists, professors, and strong government with multitudes of agencies who spent billions of dollars to deal this homeless issue for no use. In other countries which are much poorer and do not have all the wealth and advantages that we have, and we call them third world countries, they do not have homeless issues! Besides being black the homelessness is another big issue for black people because there are poorer, and they are more abounded. In every corner of our streets, we see those black homeless people with all kinds of sicknesses laying on the floor on the sidewalks. Most of the time since we are too busy, we do not notice those homeless people and look at them as another piece of rubbish on the street. For black people, this issue of homelessness is remarkably close to their hearts because too many of them are around. The homeless issue, therefore needs to be looked at as a whole and find an amicable solution for this issue. People and government should pay more attention to this issue and provide adequate housing and hospital beds and therapy centers for those homeless people.

One idea for homelessness will be (in suburbs or in a smaller town nearby) to create a beautiful park with full of amenities including nice housings with separate single quarters, grocery store, mini shopping store, a clinic, sports areas, picnicking area and finally a bus transportation to downtown and back.

JAILS FULL OF BLACKS

As we are all aware the American jails are full of black people. This phenomenon is heart ranching, beyond the reason comparing to the other nationalities. It is sad that we need to see so many blacks in our jails and thinking about it one discovers the root cause of this case. The reasons behind this case are the same as we talked about earlier meaning the color of black and the racist environment and fear of the black people. When the police see a black person in an awkward situation his presumption is that the black person is guilty, criminal, and needs to be apprehended by force and full force by use of a gun if necessary. In the same situation if the person is white then the police officer puts his guard down and he tries to comprehend the situation first before acting on it. That is one of the reasons that we have so many black American felons in jail. The other larger reason for so many black people in jails is their status in the society, black people being under suspicion and prejudices upon and discriminated all the time, therefore they do not have jobs, they are poor with broken families (with a slaves background) less education, all those contributes to their miss-behaving and acts of felony and daily encounters with a policeman, the result being jailed for any trespassing that they have done. This means, having the slave background has demoted them to fully participate in society, family and their disregard for the laws because they are always thinking those laws are to slave them more, rather than being the law-abiding citizens. Also, it does not help their condition which always they have been looked down and discriminated in finding jobs in comparison to white people. Not having jobs is forcing those black people to either stay on welfare or try to sell drugs or risk their freedom to steal even for small amounts of money or groceries etc. We as a citizen of this wonderful country, are all participants in degrading, humanizing, and providing reasons for them to act unlawfully and being jailed by suspicious minded and racist police mentally. The courts and police stations do not have proper education and training for handling black criminals. A black felon case is determined ahead of all the proven evidence.

Judges, before sentencing black felons, should really study the case not just by evidence, but by the merits and circumstances of the crime.

DRUGS TRAFFICKING

The life of a black man is conceived as a sad story with a horrendous and shameful ending. These black men, whose ancestors are slaves and he has brought up in the environment of hate, humiliation, prejudice, racist, and most of all in a world of black and white, he has become enraged and trying to survive in the world of abundance, the only thing he can do is to get involve in the gangs, drug dealing and prostitution. This black man with minimum or no education whose hands are short, his legs timid, his voice loud, and heart full of misery, punished by God and his environment, none of his making, he needs to survive…then with all these blemishes he tries to live with what he can… he steals, he sells drugs, he is in gangs, the world is a meaningless site with a journey to hell. The only way to show that he is a man and he is in control of his destination in this damn world, he become a member of gangs, gets a gun, does his drug dealing, gets involved in fights, and get harassed by police officers and eventually makes his mark on the paving with his blood all over to show his true color in red! not the black!

In our highly civilized and technological society, there should not be a place for color, discrimination, and racist attitude toward a fellow citizen. We as a society and all of the government agencies should embark on educating ourselves and our fellow citizens to care, provide for our neighbors and try to make all to progress, get an education, good jobs, look at each other's as a fellow human being with dignity and respect regardless of skin color. Millions of dollars are being spent on stupid and disastrous projects with no results, rather than spending this huge money on upbringing, helping and pushing those black citizens to improve their standing, education in society and to become equal partners in our journey in this great land of freedom and opportunity.

BLACK FAMILIES

We look at the black families as not families, but a broken-down bunch living haphazardly most of the time, no father around, no caretaker or nobody to really care about the family. Kids are brought up in the streets and they do their best to survive this injustice. Their fathers either not around, in jail, or living with another family with other siblings which they do not even know their names. Their mother tries to survive with husband gone, all alone, with few kids to nourish, she does the best she could and most of the time she succumbs to the situation; heartache, depression, damn boyfriends and society with no care. Poor kids try their best to survive the environment they are in with challenges from all around with; pimps, drug dealers, no money, and especially nobody to take care or support them, and finally, there is no one to look upon as their heroes. In such a broken family no wonder the kids cannot get proper education, the women are treated like slaves or clothes to wear whenever and wherever they need, husbands, not really! the man is jumping from bed to bed doing the best to show his manhood with no result and he is not around for too long because he is in the Ganges or in jail. In this damn society or the environment which they are, it is not wondering that nothing good prevails, nothing is accepted and prescribed a Christian family life.

Our society and government agencies need to re-consider how to deal with these broken black families and how to improve their neighborhoods and their living standards. If they are down then it is our responsibility as a whole to bring them up, provide a safe environment with good schools, reasonable jobs, and training and educating the black families in doing their best to stick together to not break up, have a bright future in mind and have models and heroes, which are shining stars for their kids.

The society, as a whole, has tremendous responsibility to help and provide guidance to those black communities and families who are discriminated and live in poverty. Kids attend those substandard schools with the worst teachers or lecturers who are not well paid and do only minimum required, rather than spend more hours with these kids to teach extra curriculum or just talk and give them advise for betterment of their lives and to direct them toward a brighter future.

MUSIC

In the devastation and the hell which black families are living through, there is a bright light which is the sound of "Music." This music comes from the heart of the ancient lands of Africa with its open spaces full of jungles, lions to roar, winds to blow, vast oceans, clean air, freedom, the song of happy African people, the melody of love and appreciation for life. Those melodies have remained in their minds and strong voices of black people which even though slaved in this new land and hindered their movements their thoughts and relationship, but they never quelled their songs. Black people are great at music and songs therefore, we have a bunch of famous songwriters, singers, and musicians who are famous worldwide. Their music comes from their heart with anguish with love and loudness which is their protest about all the injustices that they have seen and bear in the new world as grandchildren of slaves. Black musicians are very accomplished and famous all around the world with their distinct melody, rap music, blues, rock, pop, jazz, hip-hop, etc. All their music and songs are loud yet melancholy it touches hearts and souls of all people whether white or black. It tells about their downs, their pains, complaints, griefs and anger. Sometimes, their songs have vivid sounds of anger with name-calling and cussing which usually is not acceptable in other societies. They try to bring up their anger of slave-hood in their music due to their miserable life situation in the new world.

By studying those song's rethemes and meanings in them, phycologist and even people in general can detect the remnants of hardship that those black people have gone through the years of slave-hood and after.

We should do our best to understand them and while enjoying their beautiful and heart ranching music try to bring about equality and fairness toward them in our society. The black musicians should be more vocal and protest the existing condition of their people. They should be more involved in daily life of the students, by being there for them, teach them music at school after hour, have free music concerts for the kids and adolescence including preaching and lecturing them toward a productive carrier and a promise that they will have a bright future if they work hard for it.

SPORT

Sport is in the blood of every African American. Boys or Girls, at any age have this huge capacity and love for sports of many kinds, especially in basketball, football, tennis, etc. The African American youth are shining stars in their schools and college sports and athletics. They are the highest-paid athletes in the world, and they carry the respect and envy of world athletes. Athletes such as Michael Jordan, Tiger Wood, LeBron James, Koby Bryant, Serena Williams, Jesse Owens, and many others are the heroes for many white and black youths. Lots of black youth dream about and pursue couriers of those icons. That is the reason we have so many black athletes in many sports and college leagues and professional sports teams. Although, black youths are such a success in sports of any kind, in real life, most of them lack the basic education and knowhow to pursue a good life with profitable businesses or other professional jobs in many fields. This lack of enthusiasm and pursuit of education or dreams of becoming a rich businessman or a millionaire has made black families and communities to be poor and live on handouts or use of government helps such as welfare or seek other government benefits. There should be a thorough study done for the causes of this lack of enthusiasm and pursuit of education or business mentality. Is it the lack of icons for those situations or there is something else in black community that does not let them to be prosperous and wealthy citizens? We can see that black youths are excellent in sports and yet they are missing the normal living persuasions. May be they need more icons in business, education, and rich and famous so they can pursue them or, there are other elements such as the slave mentality that they have been living in and cannot free themselves from that mental confinement.

This booklet is to shed a light on the prospect of changing the mindset and culture of slavery to a mind of a free person seeking a good and prosperous life in America.

Those famous black athletes should spend some free time with school kids and adolescence to both show their care and their professional sportsmanship and meanwhile to discuss and talk about the future, which with hard work and careful study, they can make it bright and prosperous.

EDUCATION

Generally, education in American elementary and high schools are not the best in the world. Schools are mostly to keep youth in the classes and feed them till their parents come to pick them up after work. Educational books are full of pictures, but they lack in substance and real teaching for the kids. In Japan for instance, books are half the size of American teaching books, because they have less pictures, Less details and stories but they concentrate more on pertaining subject, also they ask their students to practice and memorize the lessons; being history, math or science so this way kids remember all those knowledge when they graduate from high school. Colleges and universities in US are different categories, because they teach students the best education and they are rated the highest in the world.

The sad thing is that many students especially in black communities, they do not even graduate from high school therefore, they cannot attend any colleges or universities.

There are many reasons for black youths not finishing their high school curriculums and they are dropouts. Some of the reasons are the family they come from. Those families are mostly poor, uneducated, and sadly without a father in their family to support their kids financially and emotionally. This lack of family togetherness in my opinion comes from not only being poor but also their slave-minded culture in which there were no real marriages and family togetherness, because slave owners sold slaves being men or women or kids to whomever they want regardless of their marriage or family structure. This culture, which was forced upon black families years ago has lasted even in today's black societies. Families especially parents, do not respect their marriage vows and they divorce in the slightest mood change or conditions, leaving their family without a father figure to support financially and emotionally. There are as we mentioned above other reasons such as discrimination on the job side and racist attitudes from white communities that do not let the black families to get decent jobs and live in a prosperous community. Exceptions are many but they are not the norms.

The education system in Elementary and high schools not only should be changed for the whole communities but especially should be adapted for the black communities which have underlying issues being grandchildren of slave ancestry and having to deal with the black and white issues, racism, and broken family structure. Therefore, those black students need to be thought much more than pure history and science or math but there should be phycological books to deal with their internal issues and help to get over the environment they are in.

I advocate to get a substitute teacher, parent or relative, who is educated and can help the child to study harder and the right way toward pursuing a college degree, rather than being a drop out from high school.

BLACK ICONS

African Americans should be proud of all the great black icons they have in America. Icons such as president Barak Obama and sports figures and musicians as we mentioned above and all others which we have not mention it, but they are heroes and icons for the black community and youth to look for and use as an example for their life achievements. On the other hand, to improve black communities those icons should spend time and money to encourage, to teach and improve the communities. In other hand, teachers, preachers, businessmen, entrepreneurs, and people of knowledge should spend some specific time to using their knowledge and know-how to teach the members of black communities how to improve and excel in their business and social life. They should be vigorously spent time and energy to have discussions, seminars, workplace training, meetings, and conferences about many subjects and businesses so the attendees can learn to improve their lives by those knowledge.

In schools, some phycologists should discuss the issues of race, racist behavior, how to get over the culture of slavery and change the attitude of their students to improve and be educated; not to drop out of school, not to be involved with gangs, to be patient and demanding from their parents especially from their father, to stay in the family, work with family and not to take the easy way out of divorce mentality. In black community schools, teachers should talk about the black icons, their lives, their dreams, and achievements, and most of all how they got to where they are now. Since they are role models, teachers should really talk and convince black students that by perseverance, hard work, spend many hours of studying daily and be diligent to achieve their goals and dreams. Also, they have to be role model for their siblings, so they too can have a productive and fulfilling life in the black community to try to change the fabric of their society from being poor and devastated to a community of loving families and members with dreams of equality, achievement, and no black color to stop them on reaching their goals.

Those black icons should be ready and available to meet the black families, the students and specially the college attendees, so they will hear their stories, learn from their ordeals and ups and downs of their carrier and how they accomplished their goals with hard work and determination, without paying attention to black color of their skin or looking back to their slave-hood family history.

CONCLUSION

It is my humble opinion that for African Americans to feel free, not being discriminated against, they need to change their culture of being born in a slaved society. It means that they need to feel they are fully part of America without having the stigma of slaved parents or part of the slave culture. Although, this is not a simple matter if the whole of black African American citizens come together, by way of preaching, studying, and living up to the behaviors of a free man then they could get rid of that psychology of slave-hood and inferiority. There is an other issue besides the slave mentality which is the color. Being black has created another hardship and misunderstanding for the black Americans and the color has attributed feelings of fear for the white citizens. Sadly, the history of slavery especially the slavery of the black men by white people, has a long story and this has created a culture of dominance and discrimination by white people towards black citizens which were brought to this country as slaves and they lived in plantations under yok of slavery for hundreds of years. The black people, therefore, have never been able to get rid of the slave mentality and the white Americans never tried to make is easier for the back Americans to feel free and equal to their counterparts. Hence, we have three issues to tackle: **First,** slavery itself, **Second,** the fact of being black in the white society, **Third,** the concept of pilgrimage. The **First** issue can be solved with mass reversal of culture. What I mean by this is all the new generations of the African Americans should come together and imagine that the date of the first ship landing with slaves on American shores in 1619, is actually happened **Today,** not as a slave ship, but as a free ship with free immigrants walking on the shores of America as millions of other foreigners came to this country with other ships to seek their freedom and opportunities in the land of free. This virtual concept will help the slaved people once for all to remove the yok of slavery and feel like free citizens and being equal to the rest of Americans. This concept, although seems not realistic, but I think with researchers getting involved in this practice would definitely find a way to make it happen so people can once again breathe free air and not being bounded by the culture of slavery or being associated with it. In fact, this process is almost the same as those people who go to these places of worship especially in the long distances to get strength in their faith and being born again, as many Christians and Moslems do every year by visiting holy places throughout the world such as Jerusalem and Mecca.

The **Second** condition is the skin color, to my mind, it is an absurd phenomenon created only by few governments to discriminate and pressure and rule some portion of society. The notion of white people itself is absurd. As a matter of fact, there is no "white-skinned person," there is many shades of lighter or darker skin color variety in the world. Also, in many countries, we never encounter people calling each other with the color of skins. They distinguish people through their origins or their citizenship. Therefore, it is easy to see that colonial powers and Americans use the color of the skin to further discriminate to create a feeling of helplessness, deprive those people of self-appreciation and downgrade their values and culture, exactly as the feeling created by slavery which is being not in control, weak and under pressure all the time to perform someone else's orders either right or wrong. Slave mentality means, not to think for yourself, not to be creative, not to think free and always wait for handouts or orders from someone in control. This second condition could be cured by America or other countries, to dismiss the use of skin color to refer to any citizen. A simple law can do that as is illegal to use the Nigger to call the black African Americans. Also, citizens of all the countries in the world in 21st century should be thought to respect each other regardless of their skin colors.

The **Third** condition is to vitalize and bring a new revolution to black American culture by act of Pilgriming to Africa, like Muslims go to Mecca or Christians pilgrim to Jerusalem to strengthen their faith and believes. This act or trip which could be annul or every few years, will strengthen the ties to black people in Africa and give the American blacks, the strength and spirit of a free black man or woman who never have been slaved or born to a slaved family. This association will change the thinking and spiritual wellbeing of the American blacks.

ABOUT THE AUTHOR

Oksen Babakhanian, an accomplished structural engineer who owned his consulting structural engineering business for more than thirty years. He has recently started writing few mini books after the sale of his business perusing his childhood dream of being a writer. His booklets are mostly about his experiences and world knowledge. As an engineer, he tries to enhance the social and economic situation of the society both in-home and abroad. His topics include; Rebirth of Cultural and Business Revolution in Armenia, Social Standing of African American People, Robotics and Educated Socialism System and **"The Economy of Waste"** which was published 03/08/21 by Author House.

Printed in the United States
by Baker & Taylor Publisher Services